Original title:
The Raspberry Refrain

Copyright © 2025 Creative Arts Management OÜ
All rights reserved.

Author: Helena Marchant
ISBN HARDBACK: 978-1-80586-265-9
ISBN PAPERBACK: 978-1-80586-737-1

A Bountiful Dance of Red

In a patch where laughter grows,
Berries twirl, as sunlight glows.
They tease the birds, oh what a sight,
Dancing wildly, in pure delight.

With cheeks so round and smiles so wide,
Each berry knows how to confide.
They joke with bees, in playful jest,
Sipping nectar, they feel so blessed.

Sweetness Entangled in Vines

In tangled bonds, they giggle loud,
Beneath the sun, they form a crowd.
With sugary dreams and jests to share,
These berries bloom, without a care.

They whisper secrets to the breeze,
Tickling leaves, they aim to please.
From vine to vine, they drift with glee,
A fruity plot, wild and free.

Where Berries Brush Against the Heart

In dappled light, they make a wish,
A berry's bliss, oh what a dish!
They wink at clouds, and wink at bees,
Spinning tales among the trees.

With every bite, a chuckle bursts,
Sweetness flows, quenching thirst.
They dance in bowls, atop a cream,
A fruity party, a berry dream.

Melodies Plucked from Nature's Bounty

With plump and juicy, cheeky flair,
The berries croon, without a care.
They sing of joy, in vibrant reds,
While tickling toes in grassy beds.

Each pluck a note, a sweet refrain,
Laughter ripples down the lane.
In fruity fun, they find their tune,
A symphony beneath the moon.

Savoring the Fruit of Memories

Juicy drips down on my shirt,
Hilarious mishaps in every squirt.
We laughed 'til we cried, oh what a show,
A fruit-filled mess that steals the glow.

With sticky hands we play pretend,
Each burst of flavor, a colorful blend.
In berry patches, our giggles take flight,
Dancing with shadows until the night.

The Pendant of Summer's Light

A pendant bright, with rubies aglow,
Its sparkle's a story from long ago.
We chased the sun with berry-stained hands,
And laughter spilled over, like grains of sand.

With every bite, a chuckle does burst,
Memories of summers, we quench our thirst.
We twirled and tumbled, carefree and bold,
In that pendant's shine, a tale to be told.

Harvesting Echoes of Joy

Echoes of laughter in berry-filled fields,
Harvesting giggles, the joy that it yields.
A basket of chaos, oh what a sight,
Berries and banter, all pure delight.

We'd squish and we'd squash, no need to compete,
Each mischievous nibble, a berry-filled treat.
With every sweet taste, our spirits took flight,
Harvesting echoes, oh what sheer delight.

Ruby Notes in the Afternoon

Notes of ruby glimmer in warm afternoon,
We danced to the rhythm, a silly tune.
Stomping in laughter, a berry-filled spree,
Adventures unravel, wild and free.

With shades of mischief, the sun starts to fade,
Each juicy giggle, a fanciful trade.
Moments like candy we savor with glee,
Ruby notes linger, forever carefree.

Lullabies of Red in the Night

In the garden, berries gleam,
Little creatures start to dream.
A tumbleweed rolls by with glee,
Whispering secrets, come play with me.

Cherries blush with a giggling sound,
In this realm, joy can be found.
Bumblebees dance, they hum and sway,
While moonlight teases at the end of day.

Petals and Pints in Harmony

In the pub, pints clink and cheer,
While petals float from far and near.
A toast to fruits that make us grin,
With every sip, the laughter spins.

Crimson drinks in joyful delight,
We raise our glasses to the night.
The fruits, they giggle, dance on the shelf,
Winking at us, what a mischievous elf!

A Dance with Scarlet Shadows

Underneath the crescent moon,
The shadows twirl to a silly tune.
A raspberry slips, who made that show?
With a splash of juice, it's quite the row!

The dance floor's ripe with laughter's sound,
As twinkle lights dim, we spin around.
Oh, the sprites, they leap, the joy they bring,
With every toe-tap, we're all in swing!

Echoes of Flavor in the Breeze

Breezes carry a zesty tune,
As flavors bloom from morn till noon.
A riot of berries, such cheeky fun,
With every nibble, we're never done.

Giggles travel on the breeze,
Tickling our noses with such great ease.
Flavorful whispers, they boldly tease,
Join the laughter, it's sure to please!

Melancholy Musings Among the Vines

In the garden, berries shine,
Their laughter gives me pause,
But oh, the ants march by,
In search of sticky jaws.

Beneath the leaves, I spy,
A cluster ripe and red,
Yet squirrels do not comply,
They nibble as I said.

With every twist and turn,
The vines do tease my heart,
But each berry I discern,
Is vanishing, that's art!

A pie awaits, they dream,
But crumbs fly in the breeze,
Now who will gain the cream?
With feathers on the knees!

Joyful Jingles of Nature's Bounty

There's a buzz among the leaves,
The berries sway and sing,
Jumping back from sneaky thieves,
Like it's a berry spring!

With every pluck, a giggle,
The juice it makes me dance,
Though falcons soar and wiggle,
For nectar they'll take a chance.

In this fruity paradise,
The chaos makes me grin,
A feast that's rather nice,
But I forgot my bin!

And so I pluck and stare,
At stains upon my shirt,
Who knew this bounty rare,
Would leave me in the dirt!

Vibrant Vignettes from the Wild Garden

The colors glow like laughter,
Beneath the summer sun,
Each berry tells a chapter,
Of mischief and of fun.

With vines that twist and twirl,
They tease the little bugs,
Yet laughter starts to swirl,
As I dodge their little shrugs.

I spot a sunny spread,
Their little faces beam,
But when the feast is spread,
I'm lost within a dream!

The forest sings a tune,
Of sweets and silly rhymes,
I taste the afternoon,
In sugary climbs!

Echoing Laughter of Red-Flecked Fields

The fields are full of giggles,
As berries take their flight,
They bounce in chalky wiggles,
When chased by bugs at night.

In pockets deep with joy,
They jolt with every step,
I claimed the ones to enjoy,
And danced while others crept.

With foolish falls and slips,
I trumpet each sweet bite,
But sticky fingers trips,
Will hold me through the night.

Yet laughter fills the air,
With sprouts of bright delight,
In fields where none despair,
The fuzzies take their flight!

Fragrant Notes on the Breeze

In gardens where the laughter grows,
The scent of sweet mischief flows.
A berry burst, both tart and sweet,
It tickles our toes, a fruity treat.

We dance with juice on our shirts,
Creating art with fruity flirts.
A splash of red, a dash of green,
What a sight, a berry scene!

Dewy Psalms of the Harvest

Morning dew on leaves does cling,
Whispering tales of berry bling.
We sing of jams and jellies bright,
With gooey hands, oh what a sight!

Giggling as we pluck and chase,
A raspberry throne, a berry place.
Sticky fingers, grins galore,
Out in the field, we want no more!

Ripe Rhythms Beneath the Leaves

Among the bushes, shadows play,
A berry ballet on sunny sway.
With every bite, the laughter swells,
As jokes pop out like fruity bells!

The critters join in on the fun,
As seeds fly out, we start to run.
A grinning frog, a dancing bee,
In this fruity sea, we're ever free!

A Symphony of Red and Green

In orchards where the sunbeams shine,
We whirl and twirl, those berries divine.
Crimson notes in raspberry tunes,
Strike up laughter 'neath the moons!

A goblet raised, the juice we spill,
With every sip, we get the thrill.
Frantic feet on a berry spree,
Who knew laughter grows from a tree?

Ruby Mornings and Golden Evenings

In gardens bright at early light,
The fruits hang low, a dizzying sight.
With laughter loud, we pluck and play,
A ruby feast to start the day.

As sunsets glow with golden hues,
We sip on juice, forget our blues.
The funny faces that we make,
A berry drink, for goodness' sake!

Entwined with Nature's Palette

With pockets filled, we run and dash,
To find the fruits in a joyful splash.
We muse on flavors bright and bold,
A treasure hunt, our hearts are sold.

Nature paints with colors wide,
A palette where our laughter hides.
We munch on berries, what a tease,
Each juicy burst, a giggle's breeze!

A Chorus of Bursting Delights

The summer song we sing aloud,
As berries burst, we dance so proud.
With sticky fingers, we embrace,
The sweet delight of this wild race.

A chorus leads us through the shade,
With every bite, new jokes are made.
Our giggles echo through the grove,
In berry bliss, our hearts will rove!

Chasing Shadows of Summer's Fruit

We chase the shadows, bold and free,
In search of fruits beneath the tree.
In laughter's grip, we frolic light,
With every snag, a silly sight.

The summer air, a playful breeze,
As berries bounce like buzzing bees.
A funny quest, we cannot wait,
To feast on joy, oh how great!

Veils of Velvet Berries Unfurled

In a patch where laughter blooms,
Berries dance with gummy grooms.
Velvet skins with secret charms,
Tempting fingers, wild alarms.

Jelly jars and jammy jokes,
Slippery paths where mischief pokes.
Berry stains on every shirt,
Squeaky giggles, nature's flirt.

With every bite, a juicy scream,
A tasty twist on berry dreams.
Fruits that juggle, squish, and slide,
In berry lands, we silly glide.

So raise a toast to berry fun,
Where every bite's a giggly run.
With velvet hues that never fade,
The sweetest chaos we've all made.

The Aroma of Sweet Surrender

Whiffs of sweetness fill the air,
A berry breeze, who needs a chair?
Stop and sniff, then trip and tumble,
In berry fields where giggles fumble.

The aroma lures with playful glee,
Like a puppy with its first tree.
Surrender now, just take a bite,
And giggle loud with sheer delight.

Jams of laughter, pies of cheer,
Berry gossip, loud and clear.
Scented whispers spin and swirl,
In this berry world, let joy unfurl!

With sticky hands and sticky faces,
We dance in fruit-filled, funny places.
In the garden of sweet surrender,
Laughter's fruit is our defender.

Passion Fruit and Wild Roses

In a garden where giggles bloom,
Passion fruit adds to the room.
Roses prance with joyful flair,
Spinning tales of fruity air.

Naughty petals, sweetly bold,
Tickle noses, stories told.
With nectar drips and playful sighs,
Wild berries twinkle in bright skies.

Adventures bloom with nature's zest,
Every moment feels like a jest.
Tasting fruit, we laugh anew,
In this garden, dreams come true.

With every blossom, laughter spreads,
Funny stories dance in beds.
Through wild roses, passion flies,
In berry laughter, love never dies.

Crescendo of Nature's Nectar

A symphony of berry sounds,
Nature's nectar laughs and pounds.
With every splash and juicy cheer,
We orchestrate a berry sphere.

Melodies of ripe delight,
Jingle bellies take to flight.
Harmony of tart and sweet,
Nature's rhythm, hard to beat.

Bouncing berries, chords that sing,
Fruitful frolics, joy they bring.
With giggles set to nature's tune,
We dance beneath the mocking moon.

So let us raise our spoons with pride,
To berry tunes, we'll dance and glide.
In the crescendo of pure fun,
Nature's nectar for everyone!

The Lure of Luscious Blooms

Bouncing berries on the vine,
Catch the thieves, they're doing fine.
Sneaky squirrels with clever schemes,
Nibbling snacks beneath the beams.

A bushy crown, a juicy prize,
Underneath the sunny skies.
With each bite, a giggle flows,
Funny faces as joy shows.

Frogs in tutus dance around,
While bees perform a buzzing sound.
They steal the show, they chirp and cheer,
As ripe delights draw everyone near.

In this garden, laughter swells,
A fruit parade, oh what tales it tells.
Jesters in the patch we roam,
Plucking joy, we call it home.

A Symphony of Fruit and Flight

A chorus sings from every tree,
As fruit takes flight, oh what a spree!
A berry band with drums so loud,
Drawing in a hungry crowd.

The parrot squawks, the raccoon winks,
While bees buzz close and tailor clinks.
A dance-off near the juicy patch,
All joining in—a wild match!

Giggling fruits, they swing and sway,
Juggling seeds in a fruity fray.
Cherries tumble, apples spin,
What a riot, let the games begin!

In this bazaar of zest and zest,
Nature's humor puts us to the test.
With every taste, a laugh or two,
Join the symphony, oh yes, do!

The Taste of Daydreams in Bloom

Imagining pies in a fluffy cloud,
Daydreams whisper, oh so loud.
Raspberry dreams start to unfold,
Giggles chase with flavors bold.

A sprinkle of sugar, a dash of fun,
Pies in the air, let the laughing run.
Each berry blush, a secret told,
In a patch where dreams break the mold.

The weasel winks, the hedgehog spins,
As flavors dance, where laughter wins.
Taste the sky, it tastes like glee,
In this delight, come share with me.

Flying forkfuls in a merry swirl,
Joyful chaos begins to unfurl.
With every nibble, laughter blooms,
In the sweetness of soft fruit rooms.

Echoes of Red in a Quiet Glen

In the glen where the berries play,
Laughter echoes throughout the day.
Silly shadows chase the sun,
As berries giggle, oh what fun!

Wobbling blobs in coats of red,
While dandelions nod their head.
With each bite, a silly grin,
Nature's riddle from deep within.

Caterpillars doing the twist,
As ripe delights can't be missed.
Their juicy rhymes create a beat,
With fruit-filled joy beneath our feet.

So in this glen where laughter's found,
The joyful moments spin around.
With echoes sweet of red delight,
Join the parade, it feels so right!

Crimson Echoes in the Garden

In the garden, berries twirl,
Silly squirrels begin to hurl.
They giggle as they snack and play,
Staining paws in a bright array.

Worms wearing hats frolic with glee,
While ladybugs sip tea by the tree.
The strawberries dance on a breeze,
With jelly-filled dreams and sticky keys.

Every fruit tells a cheeky tale,
Of mischief that fills the leafy trail.
Buzzing bees buzz in a comic row,
Getting lost in the juice and the glow.

The sun sets low, the shadows play,
As whispers of laughter drift away.
Beneath the moon, the garden gleams,
In hues of crimson, we dream sweet dreams.

Sweet Songs of Summer's Eve

As dusk falls down, the berries sway,
Fireflies join the stomping play.
A cat with shades struts around,
While crickets keep the funky sound.

The pie's too hot, the laughter's loud,
While ants march on, an eager crowd.
They form a band, a jolly spree,
Tap-dancing near the elder tree.

A watermelon with a grin so wide,
Whispers secrets no one can hide.
And cherries, oh, with rosy cheeks,
Share giggles through the rustling leaves.

The night grows soft, with stars above,
Echoing tunes of berry love.
Summer's tunes, they dance and weave,
In a symphony we can't believe.

Berry Whispers Beneath the Boughs

Beneath the boughs, the berries plot,
A raucous fruit party in the hot spot.
Peaches spill secrets, oh so rife,
While grapes toast to a fruity life.

A jolly rabbit hops on by,
Wearing a berry pie, oh my!
With every bounce, he leaves a trail,
Of whipped cream dreams and juicy tales.

The blackberries boast of their sweet fame,
While the elderberries play a game.
A froggy croaks tunes that make us grin,
As berries twirl in a fruited spin.

Under the moon, they giggle and sway,
In the shade where berry friends stay.
A whisper of mirth, as soft as a sigh,
Beneath the boughs, time flits by.

Lush Melodies of the Orchard

In the orchard where the apples bloom,
Dancing to a fruity tune,
The pears chuckle, plump and round,
Through every note, laughter surrounds.

A mischievous raccoon takes his chance,
Jumps into the jammy dance.
While the peaches engage in a debate,
Who's the juiciest? It's quite a fate.

The trees sway to the rhythm divine,
Strumming leaves in a playful line.
Cherries ride the breeze like pros,
Rhyming with laughter, off they go.

With a wink and a twist at every bend,
The orchard sings, it'll never end.
Nature's fun in a rainbow flow,
As melodies in the dusk brightly glow.

Reflections in a Dew-Dusted Field

In a field where dew drops glint,
A squirrel stole my berry mint.
He danced and pranced, oh what a sight,
While I laughed hard, oh what delight!

The grass was slick, I took a fall,
Chasing critters, like a fool, after all.
But with every slip and berry fling,
Came giggles pure, the joy they bring!

A buzzing bee joined in my spree,
Mocking my clumsiness with glee.
Each splash of juice, a wild delight,
Echoed laughter through the bright sunlight.

So here I rest, with nature's cheer,
In a field where nonsense is quite clear.
For every berry, a chuckle is found,
As we dance both silly and round!

Secret Lives of Lush Landscapes

Beneath the leaves, a critter's plan,
To throw a party, a berry clan!
With every bloom, a surprise awaits,
As fruits kick off their berry debates.

The hedgehogs wore their finest hats,
While rabbits danced like acrobats.
A feast arrived, oh what a sight,
With jammy jests deep into the night!

A parrot squawked with laughter profound,
"I'd never thought berries could make this sound!"
Foxes chimed in, calling shots,
They claimed the juiciest, quite the plot!

In secret glades, where shadows play,
Lush landscapes giggle, come what may.
Under the stars, they'll sing and sip,
As life's sweet laughter takes a dip!

A Tidal Wave of Berry Bliss

A wave rolled in, oh what a scene,
Made of berries, red and green!
A splash of jam and whipped cream foam,
It felt like summer, far from home.

Seagulls dived, in berry care,
While I just stood, with crumbs to share.
"Hey, stop stealing my tasty treat!
You've got your fish, now that's too sweet!"

The ocean giggled, the tide would rise,
As berries danced beneath the skies.
Each wave that crashed brought bursts of cheer,
I splashed and sang, oh what a year!

In this berry sea, with friends galore,
We laughed and played, forevermore.
As the sun dipped low, we'd reminisce,
About that wave, that juicy bliss!

Harmonics of Savory and Sweet

Oh what a mix, the savory sweet,
A chorus of flavors we all must greet!
With cheese that giggles and jams that hum,
Together they dance, oh how they strum!

The brie flew high, on a toasty bread,
While berry tarts just danced ahead.
"Join us now for a grand duet,
With laughter and flavors, we won't forget!"

Carrots twirled in a fancy jig,
While berries burst, oh so big!
The harmony rang through field and glade,
As every tastebud happily swayed.

So when you nibble on life's great feast,
Remember this dance, a savory beast.
For in every munch, a tune reveals,
A fruity giggle, that joy conceals!

A Collection of Scarlet Dreams

In a patch on the hill, bright berries burst,
Their laughter in fields, oh, how they burst!
With each little nibble, a giggle pops out,
As juice paints our faces, swirling about.

Chasing the critters who sneak with a grin,
Berry bandits dance, let the picking begin!
Miracle fruits, with a playful taunt,
A tickle on taste buds, oh, what a jaunt!

Sticky sweet fingers, it's a colorful game,
Each berry a prank, each flavor, a name,
Around us, they plot in their red, shiny dress,
Nature's own jesters, we're laughing, no less.

With baskets we roam, under skies so wide,
A parade of giggles on this sweet berry ride,
These scamps of the summer, what fun they create,
In a field full of mischief, we're never too late!

Whispers of Sun-Kissed Shores

On sandy stretches, berries wild and free,
Waves crash as seagulls join in the spree.
Under sun's warm gaze, we all leap and dive,
With berries in hand, oh, we feel so alive!

Laughter in air, as we chase after snacks,
A tide of red treasures, we fill in our packs.
Each juicy morsel, a splash of delight,
As shadows grow long, we dance into the night.

Playful waves giggle, they tickle our toes,
While we feast like kings, as the sunset glows.
Stories of pirates, of legends and lore,
With each berry bite, we're explorers once more.

Dancing to rhythms of laughter and fun,
Berry hats donned, we're all under one sun.
Whispers of summer tickle our dreams,
In this fruity haven, nothing's as it seems!

The Allure of Nature's Abundance

In gardens so lush, where the silliness reigns,
Berries burst forth, like sweet little chains.
We dip them in chocolate, we wear them as crowns,
Competing with squirrels; it's a game with no frowns.

With a wink at the sky, the sun gives a cheer,
As we scurry about, spreading joy far and near.
The fruits of our labor, they puff out with pride,
Ripe for the picking, in nature we ride.

Sipping on smoothies, we giggle and sway,
Each sip brings a chuckle, brighten up the day.
Conspiring with daisies, sharing the fun,
With each tiny berry, laughter is spun.

As twilight descends, our merry crew sings,
In fields full of wonder, laughter takes wings.
Nature's abundance, a treasure to share,
With berries at sunset, joy fills the air!

Tangy Tales Under the Stars

Under a blanket of twinkling delight,
Berries roll free, dancing in moonlight.
Sipping on juices, we burst into rhyme,
With each tangy tale, we're losing all time.

A mischievous raccoon joins our late-night feast,
Sampling our berries, a curious beast.
With jokes in the air and laughter galore,
Spilled juice on our shirts, but we always want more.

We tell tales of fairies who steal fruit at dawn,
Of adventurous nights that stretch out till yawn.
These berries the stars, shining bright on our lips,
As we savor the sweetness with giggles and sips.

Under the cosmos, with whimsies to share,
Each bite is a giggle, without a single care.
In this world of enchantment where berries are kings,
We dance 'neath the moon to the joy that it brings!

The Secret Symphony of Summer

In the garden, giggles play,
Berries bouncing in the sun's rays.
Juicy tunes dance on my tongue,
Summer's orchestra has begun!

Silly squirrels join the song,
Cartwheeling where they don't belong.
Under leaves, a messy feast,
Berry chaos, to say the least!

Lemonade laughter fills the air,
Sticky fingers with not a care.
Sun hats tilt and slips occur,
Every bite's a joyful slur!

Berry capers in the heat,
Nature's pranks can't be beat.
As the season starts to fade,
Memories of mischief made!

Enchanted Breaths of Berry Dreams

Once upon a berry patch,
Dreams of sweetness, what a catch!
Bubblegum clouds float up high,
Kites and laughter fill the sky.

Berry bandits try to steal,
Each juicy bite, a tasty meal.
With every pick, we spill and trip,
A fruity frenzy, a berry slip!

Crimson smiles and purple grins,
Sticky faces where fun begins.
Giggles echo through the fields,
Nature's magic, laughter yields!

Running wild, we make a mess,
Sun-kissed moments, we confess.
As twilight whispers, dreams take flight,
In berry wonder, pure delight!

An Ode to Summer's Sweetest Gift

Oh, what joy in every bite,
Berry treasures, pure delight!
A taste of sunshine on my tongue,
Songs of summer to be sung.

Plump and ripe, they splash and squirt,
Red-stained fingers and sun-kissed shirt.
With each giggle, drops do fall,
Berry bliss, we've got it all!

Grandma's recipe, a juicy pie,
Filling dreams beneath the sky.
Friends unite, we laugh and cheer,
Slice of summer, we hold dear!

But watch out for the sneaky bees,
Buzzing 'round with berry breeze.
In this sweet and funny mess,
We find our joy, we must confess!

The Hidden Treasures of Earth's Bounty

Treasure maps lead us astray,
To hidden fruits, a berry ballet.
Brownie points for tasty finds,
Berries twist in playful binds!

Mischief brews under leafy green,
Jelly jars and roads unseen.
Pies and jams, a wild assortment,
Laughter's juice, our sweet endorsement!

Popping berries, oh, what fun,
Creating chaos in the sun.
With each scoop, our smiles grow,
In berry love, we steal the show!

Ready, set, let's make a mess,
Nature's gift, we must confess.
So here we gather, without a doubt,
In every berry, laughter shouts!

Juicy Verses in the Morning Mist

In the garden, birds convene,
Nibbles on berries, oh so keen!
Chattering squirrels dance with glee,
While morning fog hugs every tree.

A slippery berry, dropped with flair,
Rolls down the path, what a scare!
Chasing after, laughter flows,
Feet in the mud, oh, how it shows!

Sticky fingers, a sweet delight,
Biting into joy feels just right.
Giggles shared in morning's glow,
With every berry, spirits grow!

Nature's prankster, ripe and bold,
With giggly tales that never grow old.
In the mist, we find our play,
Berry mischief, come what may!

Scarlet Serenades at Twilight

Underneath the waning light,
Raspberry shadows dance in flight.
Bees hum tunes, both loud and sweet,
As critters gather for a treat.

Giggling hedgehogs roll about,
Berry juice is what they tout.
A melody of juicy fun,
Beneath the stars, we're never done!

Mice in tuxedos, sipping fine,
Champing on scraps, their favorite dine.
The twilight sounds are quite a show,
While heartbeats sync with every glow!

Creamy clouds in a purple sky,
As ants march in, oh me, oh my!
A serenade of crimson cheer,
With berries bursting, fun is near!

Nature's Lullaby of Sunlit Fields

In sunlit fields, where berries sway,
Nature hums a playful lay.
Frolicking frogs croak on cue,
While dandelions dance anew.

A bumblebee drops by for tea,
With petals stuck, oh what a spree!
Raspberries wear a cheeky grin,
Offering treats to share within.

The grassy sea sways in a blur,
As kids chase after little fur.
Laughter echoes, wild and free,
Berries tumble, oh look at me!

Even the sun seems to smile,
As we munch and laugh for a while.
Nature sings its sweet refrain,
While berries promise joy in gain!

The Taste of Wild Harmony

An orchestra of colors bright,
Under the sky, a joyful sight.
Berries twirl in a fruity dance,
Inviting all to join the prance.

Frogs in tuxes claim their place,
As crickets serenade the space.
A raccoon stirs, with paws so sly,
Swiping fruit, oh me, oh my!

Dew-kissed petals, sweetly worn,
As morning stretches, new and torn.
We laugh and sing, our cups held high,
A taste of wild beneath the sky!

With every bite, a giggle shared,
In nature's arms, we're never scared.
This harmony of fun we chase,
In berry fields, we find our place!

The Artistry of Harvested Hues

Beneath the sun, they wiggle and shine,
Ripe reds and greens, they mock the divine.
Pies and jams, oh what a sight,
Nature's joke, served up just right.

Laughter erupts as berries collide,
In baskets they tumble, they take a ride.
Juicy tales as fingers get stained,
Oh, the fun when summer is gained.

The squirrels dance, oh what a show,
Stealing treats, putting on a glow.
Fields of color, voices so loud,
Nature's festival, drawing a crowd.

But watch your step, they squish with glee,
Epic fails, oh can't you see?
Berry-stained antics, smiles all around,
In the artistry where joy is found.

Lyrical Fruits in a Golden Hour

In golden light, the fruits all sing,
Mischief and giggles, such a thing!
The chorus sweet, with a hint of jest,
Dancing along, they're surely blessed.

Jams and jellies, sticky delight,
Hands flailing 'round, oh what a sight!
A fruit-filled party, oh so divine,
Each round of laughter tastes so fine.

Chasing shadows and beetles nearby,
As berries pop, the giggles fly high.
A melody of flavors, both sweet and bold,
Stories unfold, forever retold.

But mind the pie, it's cheekily warm,
Bouncing around, it's part of the charm.
Colors explode in playful display,
In this fruity dance, we surely will stay.

Crimson Echoes in the Garden

In the garden, whispers do reign,
Crimson echoes, who can contain?
Bouncing berries sing a cheer,
"Eat us now, or we disappear!"

Watch them wiggle, full of sass,
Running riot, what a class!
Squished between toes, an oops or two,
Berry-fueled giggles, oh who knew?

With splashes of color, the world is bright,
Each round of laughter, pure delight.
Birds join the chorus, flapping their wings,
In this garden, where joy simply swings.

But beware the ants, cunning and sly,
They march in ranks, no reason why.
In playful chaos, the harvest unfolds,
With these crimson echoes, adventure holds.

Sweet Whispers of Summer's Kiss

In the summer sun, a sweet tease,
Whispers of berries float on the breeze.
Each bite a giggle, a playful jest,
Beneath the leaves, we're truly blessed.

Baskets overflowing, jam sessions await,
Every spoonful brings tales in our fate.
A berry bonanza, laughter in waves,
Our sticky fingers, oh how it saves!

Squeals of delight as fruits tumble down,
Childlike joy, in sun-kissed crown.
The taste of mischief, bold and bright,
As we dance in the garden, pure delight.

But look out, oh birds with beady eyes,
They swoop and swirl, oh what a surprise!
In this sweet summer's kiss, we'll play,
With laughter and berries, come what may.

Ruby Melodies Under the Moon

Beneath the moon, they start to sing,
The berries bounce, oh what a fling!
With giggles high and laughter bright,
They dance around in pure delight.

A squirrel joins, his tail a blur,
He shakes his hips, a furry stir!
In rhymes of red and jests so sweet,
Their night is filled with berry treat.

Jelly jars, a juggling game,
The ants all cheer and call their names!
With every slip and juicy burst,
These merry pals, they laugh and thirst.

So here's to nights of berry fun,
With laughter loud, we're never done!
In ruby hues, we spin and twirl,
Under the moon, we dance and whirl.

Berry-Laden Dreams at Dusk

As dusk arrives, dreams start to play,
The berries whisper in a playful way.
A patch of dreams, a jester's laugh,
They plot a scheme, a berry craft.

With hats of leaves and smiles so wide,
They tickle each other, no place to hide.
The bushes giggle, the breeze assists,
In this berry world, none can resist.

Dreams of jam and jelly spills,
With slippery giggles and berry thrills.
They make a mess, oh what a sight,
As berries bounce in fading light.

So let us dream with juicy flair,
As berry giggles fill the air.
In this berry-laden land of cheer,
We laugh aloud, the end is near!

Juicy Secrets Beneath the Leaves

Beneath the leaves, the chatter grows,
Juicy secrets, everyone knows.
With winks and whispers, they share their tales,
Of shiny fruits and playful gales.

A berry busts, it squirts with glee,
And stains the toes of a giggly bee.
With silly prances and tales so absurd,
They sing of adventures, all unheard.

The frogs applaud with leaps and croaks,
While crickets join with silly jokes.
In juicy lands, where laughter streams,
They find delights in berry dreams.

With secrets held so close each night,
These berry pals create pure fright.
The laughter echoes, wild and free,
Beneath the leaves, come join with me!

A Serenade of Scarlet Hues

In scarlet hues, the berries play,
Their serenade brightens up the day.
With bouncing notes and tunes so sweet,
They bring the sun to dance with feet.

The jolly blooms all twirl around,
With petal-friends hopping to the sound.
A berry ball, they spin and laugh,
Each twirl a giggle, a joyful craft.

A dance-off starts, who'll win the crown?
With every stumble, they tumble down.
Yet in their falls, they find their glee,
In scarlet hues, they sing carefree.

So let us join this merry dance,
And weave the colors, make a chance.
In serenades of berry charm,
We laugh aloud, no reason for alarm!

A Tangle of Nature's Richness

In the garden, berries bloom,
Like confetti, Nature's room.
Silly squirrels dance with glee,
Eating fruit like it's a spree.

Laughing bees buzz all around,
Tickled by the sweetness found.
Jelly jars, they take a dive,
In this feast, we feel alive.

A fuzzy hat upon my head,
Worn for fun, not for the bread.
Nature's bounty, what a treat,
Berries tasty, can't be beat!

Chasing shadows, giggles play,
In this colorful buffet.
Each bite brings a burst of joy,
Nature's candy we employ.

Serendipity in Silken Berries

Beneath the sun, oh what a find,
Berries winking, so unconfined.
A pink explosion on my toes,
When I step where sweet vine grows.

The puppy joins, his tongue all red,
Drooling hapless, joy widespread.
Berries bouncing, playful treat,
Nature's mischief, oh so sweet!

A splash of juice, a silly stain,
On my shirt, it's all in vain.
With laughter echoing around,
Nature's treasure, sweetly crowned.

Sticky fingers, giggling crew,
Every taste a funny view.
Silken drips, we leap and cheer,
In berry land, there's nothing here!

The Garden's Sweet Serenade

In the garden, colors play,
Berries brightening up the day.
Frogs in hats, they croak and hop,
While dancing flies just never stop.

A frosty spoon, the feast begins,
Pouring jam, oh where's the sins?
Silly hats atop our heads,
Laughing out while jelly spreads!

A breeze that tickles, birds that sing,
Make my heart do a happy fling.
With each wink of berry bright,
Spreading joy, oh what a sight!

Twisting twirls in nature's song,
Where the flavors all belong.
Sweet serenade in the sun,
Happiness grows, we've just begun!

A Canvas of Flavor and Fragrance

In vibrant hues, a canvas spread,
Juicy colors dance ahead.
With laughter like a painter's brush,
Berry splashes cause a hush.

Splotchy shoes and painted hats,
The silliest of all the chats.
In a world where flavors roam,
Every berry feels like home.

Tickling noses, sweet delights,
Chasing giggles in the flights.
A jam that winks, a pie that sings,
Nature's laughter, joy it brings!

So let's engage in this grand play,
With fruity dreams, we'll drift away.
In joyful chaos, we will stay,
Creating art in berry's sway!

A Harvest of Stardust and Sunshine

In gardens lush where colors bloom,
I tripped on vines, what a doom!
With laughter bright, I picked away,
A berry feast to start my day.

The sunbeams danced on every berry,
While bees buzzed close, oh what a merry!
I juggled fruits, a clumsy show,
And squished one good, now it won't go!

A picnic planned, with snacks in tow,
But ants adorned my board—oh no!
They joined the feast, how bold they be,
A shared delight, just them and me!

With every bite, a giggle shows,
Bright red stains where the laughter flows.
Each fruity joke, a punchline sweet,
In sunshine's glow, life's little treat!

Symphony of Sweetness in a Glass

A blender whirred, a Berry Bash,
With splashes bright and seeds to crash.
I poured my mix, a colorful stream,
But accidentally made a cream!

The dance of flavors, oh so grand,
With every sip, I took a stand.
Straws flew out like wild balloons,
While fruit danced to peculiar tunes!

A misfit blend of odd delight,
Coconut flakes took flight in flight!
I raised my glass with childish cheer,
Sipped in joy and felt no fear!

Each tiny burst, a laughter spark,
A fruity joke from dawn till dark.
It drips and spills, a sweet parade,
In sticky bliss, my worries fade!

Rhapsody of Nature's Palette

In fields of green, I took a stroll,
Berries bright, my heart's console.
A brush of hues, nature's own play,
A colorful scene to light my day.

The reds and blues began to chat,
A sweet debate on who was fat!
With a chuckle loud, they took a stand,
Each fruit proclaiming it's the grand!

A plump blue gem said with a grin,
"I'm juicy, take me for a spin!"
While rosy reds sang notes of fun,
"Without me here, you'd come undone!"

With every bite, I joined the song,
In nature's choir, I felt so strong.
Laughter echoed through the trees,
Joyful moments, a berry breeze!

A Tapestry of Taste and Time

In a kitchen bright with jars galore,
I mixed and stirred, oh what a chore!
With splashes of juice, a chaotic scene,
A tapestry woven with flavors keen.

My grandmother's recipe whispered sweet,
As I danced around with clumsy feet.
The timer pinged, a joyful sound,
I opened the door, my treasure found!

But oh, what a mess I had beheld,
With fruit explosions that proudly yelled!
A sticky floor, a berry blast,
With giggles ringing, my fun amassed!

Each spoonful served, a memory made,
With friends and laughs, my heart displayed.
In every jar, a story shines,
A taste of joy through silly times!

Silken Tones of a Berry Bramble

In the bramble where berries bloom,
A squirrel sings, making quite the room.
His voice is sweet, a berry's tease,
While bees join in with laughter and ease.

Frogs croak back with sarcastic cheer,
Chasing shadows, they leap and appear.
The fruits chuckle as they dangle high,
Giggling softly, 'Oh, my oh my!'

A hedgehog sways, his dance a spree,
Trying to keep up with the berry spree.
With every step, the fruits burst bright,
As critters twirl in pure delight.

Underneath the sun, a wild affair,
Bramble parties, without a care.
Let's savor this silly, absurd delight,
As berries laugh through day and night.

Vivid Stanzas Underneath the Sun

The sun shines down on a berry patch,
Where rabbits gamble and plan to hatch.
With every hop, they trade a pun,
In the bright ballet of berry fun.

Bluebirds chirp in harmony sweet,
While ladybugs dance on their tiny feet.
They spin tales of jams and pies,
Leaving all nearby in fits of sighs.

Mice play tricks with a feathery plume,
Twirling around like they own the room.
Each berry blushes, blushing so red,
As laughter bubbles, joy is widespread.

With every giggle, the day drips gold,
Nature's rhapsody, never grows old.
In vivid stanzas, life takes its run,
Beneath the sun, it's all just fun!

Honeyed Chimes from the Berry Patch

In the patch, where sweetness abounds,
Bumblebees buzz with giggling sounds.
They carry tunes of pure delight,
While butterflies flutter from morning to night.

Each berry hangs, like notes on strings,
Swaying lightly with the joy it brings.
The wind whispers secrets, juicy and sweet,
As critters convene for a dance of their feet.

A goat strums gently on a twig so fine,
While ants march rhythm, in single line.
With every strum, radiant colors bloom,
Amidst the laughter, a life that's in tune.

As honey drips from trees so grand,
The berry patch becomes a band.
With honeyed chimes that uplift the air,
Flavors mix joyfully in nature's fair.

Whispered Secrets of the Forest Floor

On the forest floor, where stories unfold,
Mushrooms giggle, secrets to hold.
The wind rustles leaves, like a gossiping friend,
Chirping tales of berries around the bend.

Twirling around, the crickets stay late,
Cheering the mishaps they create.
A dance-off erupts under moon's soft glow,
With twigs as grand prizes, just for show.

Down by the streams, frogs croon in dusk,
Making light of a dragonfly's fuss.
Each leap is a laughter, each splash is a joke,
A symphony of chuckles, with each little poke.

The night's a canvas, painted in fun,
With whispers and laughter, they all run.
In the forest's embrace, all cares are forgot,
Where joy is abundant, and laughter is caught.

Petals and Phrases in Bloom

In a garden so bright, laughter flies,
The petals tell jokes, oh what a surprise!
Bees wear bow ties, buzzing along,
While daisies hum tunes, a merry song.

Sunflowers dance, with a sway and a grin,
They spin about wildly, let the fun begin!
With every bright color, smiles take their flight,
Nature's own party, a pure delight!

Ladybugs chuckle, their laughter so sweet,
In crisp autumn air, they tap dance their feet.
A butterfly jokes, with a wink and a twirl,
In petals and phrases, we all start to whirl.

So come join the fun, let the giggles zoom,
In this vibrant space, life begins to bloom!
With humor and joy, every heart will see,
Petals of laughter, so wild and free.

Luscious Lyrical Landscapes

In a berry patch bright, songs take their flight,
With blueberries laughing, a pure appetite.
Raspberries giggle, as they sway in the breeze,
Their juicy jokes carried with grace through the trees.

Strawberries shout, with a splash of delight,
'We're the sweetest of all, join our tasty flight!'
With a wink and a grin, they dance on their vines,
Creating a symphony, where laughter entwines.

Blackberries bounce, in their charming parade,
While the wild winds whisper sweet jokes they've made.
A chorus of flavors, a playful brigade,
In luscious landscapes, where fun is displayed.

So gather the fruit, let the laughter ignite,
In these lyrical lands, we're feeling just right!
With joy in each nibble, and smiles that expand,
Life's delectable rhythm, a playful stand.

Fruitful Dreams in a Woodland

In a woodland so lush, dreams play hide and seek,
With squirrels in hats, oh, they're quite unique!
Cherries in giggles, dangle from trees,
While mushrooms are chortling, shaking their leaves.

Wandering through paths lined with ripe, juicy fare,
Peaches share puns with the wise, old hare.
'Don't be a prude,' winks the mischievous plum,
'In this fruity land, we have fun that's humdrum!'

In shadows and sun, the laughter cascades,
Berries unite, forming giggling parades.
Blue jays do stand-up, their jokes very keen,
Nature's own stage, where joy takes the screen.

So venture right here, into this sweet dance,
Where fruits weave their wit, join the playful romance!
In fruitful dreams, with each chuckle so bright,
The woodland is bursting with pure, vivid light.

Nectarous Narratives of Joy

In the hive of delight, stories take flight,
Honeybees buzz, with all of their might.
'Once upon a time,' they cheerfully hum,
'In sweet nectar lands, where laughter's no fun!'

With honeycombs polished, they spin tales so grand,
Of fruits that did wonder, in this bustling band.
A berry once joked, with a twist and a spin,
'I'm more than a snack, I'm the laughter within!'

The flowers all gathered, their petals aflame,
Each short little story, a song with a name.
The breeze carried giggles, through fields full of cheer,
In nectarous tales, there's nothing to fear!

So share in the joy, let the sweetness unfold,
With narratives vibrant and laughter so bold.
In this merry patch, with stories to share,
Life's nectarous moments are beyond compare!

Adventures in a Berry-Strewn Path

Once I walked a berry trail,
Where fruits were ripe and never pale.
I tripped on jam, oh what a mess,
And laughed at berry-stained distress.

A squirrel eyed my berry stash,
I chased it down with quite a splash.
It darted off with berry cheer,
While I just stood, a bit austere.

The birds sang songs of fruity glee,
As I gave chase, but they flew free.
I vowed to catch a berry thief,
But got distracted by my grief.

With every step, a juicy slip,
These berry antics made me trip.
I'll never learn, I'll take my stand,
To berry-folly, I'm quite a fan.

Tender Threads of a Sweet Harvest

In fields of red, I came to play,
With raspberries bright to light my day.
I picked a handful, oh what fun,
Until I found an angry nun.

She waved her arms, said, 'Leave those be!'
But berry juice got on my knee.
I laughed and danced, 'What's the big deal?'
While she just shook her head with zeal.

With every bite, a squishy thrill,
The laughter growing louder still.
Each berry burst, a merry prank,
A sweet delight, my fun-filled bank.

I climbed a bush, my berry throne,
With laughter echoing through the groan.
And all around, the harvest sweet,
Was just a game, a berry feat.

The Allure of Juicy Secrets

Oh what a secret berries keep,
In every bush, surprises creep.
I found a treasure, what a shock,
A cheeky gnome stole my stock!

I chased him down, my heart a race,
Through strawberry patches, what a chase!
He giggled loud, his cap askew,
"Catch me if you can!" he flew.

With slippery feet and sticky hands,
We zigged and zagged in berry lands.
He made a splash, then danced around,
With berries raining on the ground.

I finally caught him, what a sight!
We shared the spoils in pure delight.
Juicy secrets now revealed,
In laughter's grip, our fates congealed.

Crimson Whispers on the Wind

Breezes sang of berry dreams,
As I devised my berry schemes.
I'd wear a crown of juicy hues,
And dance around like I had views.

The rabbits cheered, a jolly band,
While I proclaimed, 'This is quite grand!'
With every stomp, a berry burst,
A sweet rebellion, oh the thirst.

But shock! A bear, my foe in jest,
Appeared to spoil my berry fest.
He grinned and took my crown with glee,
Said, "Join me, friend, let's sip some tea!"

So off we went, two unlikely mates,
In berry patches, sharing plates.
Crimson whispers, laughter infuse,
In berry lands, we'll never lose.

Tantalizing Rhapsody of Summer's End

In hues of red beneath the sun,
The merry feast has just begun.
With sticky hands and laughter bright,
We dance around in pure delight.

A berry here, a squishy mess,
Each bite's a riddle, I confess.
The juice drips down like summer rain,
And giggles echo, sweet and plain.

The squirrels take part in our charade,
They sneak a snack, then quickly fade.
While we parade in berry-tied,
The moments shared won't be denied.

As twilight casts a sleepy spell,
We toast to summer, bid farewell.
With every chuckle, every cheer,
These bouncy days, we hold so dear.

Crimson Harmonies on a Meadow's Edge

Upon the hill, we gather round,
With cheeky smiles that knows no bound.
Each plump delight we pluck with glee,
A berry chorus, wild and free.

The laughter twirls in berry-stained,
Our treasure hunts, forever gained.
With petals soft, the breeze will sing,
Of fruity joys and everything.

But watch your step, a berry's deed,
Can turn a romp to berry greed.
As thunder rolls, we rise and flee,
While stains of joy drip down from me.

At sunset's glow, we wave goodbye,
To summer's end and playful sighs.
In shadows long, we reminisce,
Of berry games we can't dismiss.

Enchanted Grove of Tasting Whispers

In shaded nooks, the secrets dwell,
With fruity bites, it's like a spell.
The laughter hides in every leaf,
A playful prank, beyond belief.

We nibble close, a sneaky treat,
As critters join the fruity feat.
With wobbly grins, we slip and slide,
In berry bliss, our joy won't hide.

The sun peeks through, a glistening ray,
While berry stains lead us astray.
Each giggle shared in nature's grace,
Turns every moment into a race.

With every laugh, our hearts combine,
In secret groves, oh how we shine.
As summer fades, we hold on tight,
To every berry, every night.

Silhouette of a Berry-Stained Dream

A field of dreams where laughter leads,
We twirl and swirl among the reeds.
With purple tongues and berry bliss,
We trap the sun, can't miss a kiss.

The shadows dance beneath the trees,
As berries hang like memories.
A tangle of joy, a splash of shade,
In every giggle, plans we've made.

Oh, berry stains on shirts and hands,
A gallery of summer's bands.
With friends beside, we wander free,
Through laughter's lens, our spirits' spree.

When night arrives, the crickets hum,
While we sit back, our hearts go thrum.
With berry tales that twist and sway,
We dream of summer's grand array.

Notes from the Briar Patch

In a patch where berries tumble,
A squirrel stole one — took a fumble.
He danced about in berry glee,
As juice dripped down to meet a bee.

A hedgehog joined the berry feast,
With all his prickles, he's a beast.
They laughed and giggled, oh what fun!
In the briar patch, we all were one.

The herbs all whispered, 'What a sight!'
As birds kept chirping with delight.
A chatty crow flew by with flair,
And dropped a berry in my hair.

So if you wander near that patch,
Expect the laughter — it's a match.
The berries tell a tale, you see,
Of funny frolics, wild and free.

Wandering Through Ruby Fields

Oh, wandering through the fields so bright,
Where berries gleam like gems in light.
I spy a rabbit with a grin,
Who hoards his hoard of berries thin.

He hops around, a berry thief,
Each jump a burst of comic relief.
With one in paw, he starts to prance,
While birds above join in the dance.

A snake slid by with quite a flair,
But tumbled into a berry chair.
He slithered off with bits of red,
Declaring, "I'll eat till I'm fed!"

So join this parade of berry fun,
Where laughter rolls and jokes are spun.
In ruby fields, all joy abounds,
With every berry, humor found.

Dreams Dripping in Crimson

In dreams that drip with crimson hues,
A pig adorned in berry shoes.
He trotted down the laughing lane,
With berries plastered on his brain.

A crow cawed out, "What a sight!"
As piggy danced with all his might.
He slipped and slid, then took a dive,
And rolled in berries, sweet and alive.

The cows all mooed, "What a scene!"
As berries splattered, so serene.
With laughter rising to the skies,
They chewed on tales that made them fly.

So feast your eyes on dreams so bright,
Where joy and fruit unite in flight.
In every drop of crimson play,
A funny story finds its way.

Sunlit Sonnet of the Orchard

In the orchard bathed in golden light,
Where laughter spills with sheer delight.
A cat in shades lounges so fine,
Dreams of berries and sun-warmed wine.

He spots a mouse, a berry fiend,
With little paws, he's keen and green.
They dance around the apple trees,
Chasing shadows in the soft breeze.

A lively dog joins in the chase,
With berry stains upon his face.
They twist and twirl, a merry band,
In orchards filled with fruit so grand.

So roam the sunlit paths and cheer,
Where every berry brings a tear.
In this sonnet with a playful twist,
Each fruity laugh you can't resist.

Juiced Lullabies of the Grove

In the grove where berries swing,
Laughter drips, and joy takes wing.
A squirrel dances on a vine,
Chasing acorns, feeling fine.

The sun's a pie, the sky's a tease,
Berries bouncing in the breeze.
A jester's hat for garden sprites,
They giggle through the summer nights.

With every berry, giggles flow,
Who knew such fun could grow so slow?
A sprig of mint with wicked leer,
Tells gusty tales for all to hear.

So come and taste the silly spree,
Join the dance, take it from me.
Underneath the berry shade,
Let's sip the fun the grove has made.

bursting with Berries and Bliss

Berries burst with cheeky glee,
Juicy notes for you and me.
A thicket filled with sweet delight,
We chase the sun, we chase the light.

Comical critters roll around,
Beneath the plants, their laughter's found.
With every bite, a giggle grows,
In berry land, anything goes.

The pie is won by a bumbling bee,
He wears a crown, as proud as can be.
Flavors whirling in a dance,
Berry madness, take a chance!

So join the feast of sweetened cheer,
With each plump berry, bring good cheer.
Let's ruffle leaves, and twirl in jest,
In this garden, we are blessed.

Garden of Temptation and Taste

In gardens where the strawberries sing,
Every berry wears a quirky bling.
A wiggly worm with a radish hat,
Jumps in joy, oh, imagine that!

Sweet temptation lies in wait,
As giggles float through every gate.
A blueberry grins with mischief set,
Calling everyone, "Don't you fret!"

They dance like fools on a sunny day,
Berry breezes joining in the play.
A cherry's wink, a raspberry grin,
In this garden, we're all kin.

Taste the laughter, sip the fun,
Berry banter has begun.
In this patch, let's paint the air,
With sweet delights beyond compare!

Whispers Wrapped in Berry Bliss

Whispers weave through leafy threads,
Tickling tummy laughs and spreads.
A buzzing bee with a berry tale,
Tells of joy down the viney trail.

Blueberries bounce in a merry race,
Laughter sprinkles every space.
A cheeky crow with a pie in tow,
Cackles loud, "Don't take it slow!"

Nature's giggles and fruity charms,
Wrap us up in grinning arms.
With every nibble, a jolt of cheer,
Berry bliss is finally here!

So join the brawl of berry fun,
Under the sun, let's all run.
With whispers soft and laughter bright,
We'll feast on joy through day and night.

www.ingramcontent.com/pod-product-compliance
Lightning Source LLC
Chambersburg PA
CBHW070008300426
43661CB00141B/370